Delicious Slow Cooker Plant Based Diet Cookbook

An Irresistible Collection of Vegetable Recipes for Your Slow Cooker

BY: SOPHIA FREEMAN

© 2021 Sophia Freeman All Rights Reserved

COPYRIGHTED

Liability

This publication is meant as an informational tool. The individual purchaser accepts all liability if damages occur because of following the directions or guidelines set out in this publication. The Author bears no responsibility for reparations caused by the misuse or misinterpretation of the content.

Copyright

The content of this publication is solely for entertainment purposes and is meant to be purchased by one individual. Permission is not given to any individual who copies, sells or distributes parts or the whole of this publication unless it is explicitly given by the Author in writing.

Table of Contents

Introduction 6

Additional Useful & Interesting Information 8

    Stuffed Peppers 9

    Artichoke & Spinach Dip 12

    African Sweet Potato Stew 15

    Moroccan Chickpea Stew 18

    Pumpkin & Chickpea Curry 21

    Slow Cooked Pinto Beans 24

    Mixed Root Veggie Stew 27

    Cauliflower Soup 30

    Jackfruit 34

    Vegetarian Chili 38

    Vegetable Jambalaya 41

    Apple Butter 44

    Eggplant Lasagna 46

    Slow Cooked Black Beans 50

    Tofu Tikka Masala 53

    Butternut Squash Soup 57

    Tortilla Lasagna 60

    Vegetable Buffalo Dip 63

Spiced Acorn Squashes 66

Slow Cooked Broccoli 69

Mushroom Marsala 72

Slow Cooker Baked Potatoes 75

Sweet Potato Stew with Lentils 78

Chickpea Tagine 81

Sweet & Savory Beans 85

Butternut Squash & Whole Grains 88

Enchilada Pie 91

Minestrone 95

Spicy Ham, Lentil & Chickpea Stew 99

Butternut Squash & Cinnamon Soup 102

Feta Cheese Dip 106

Italian Squash 109

Vegetables & Beans 112

Cheesy Spinach 115

Sweet Potatoes with Walnuts & Maple 118

Potato Soup 121

Cheesy Creamed Corn 124

Stuffed Onions 127

Barbecue & Salsa Beans 130

Garlic Mashed Potatoes with Herbs 133

Lemon Spring Veggies 136

White Bean & Spinach Soup 139

Pumpkin Soup with Lentils 142

Slow Cooked Green Beans & Carrots 145

Praline Sweet Potatoes 148

Artichoke Cream Dip 151

Split Pea Soup 154

Bulgur & Beans 157

Mexican Fondue 161

Cauliflower Korma 164

Conclusion 167

Author's Afterthoughts 168

Introduction

A plant-based diet is an eating pattern that is primarily composed of vegetables, fruits, whole grains, legumes, beans, seeds and nuts. It puts emphasis on the consumption of whole foods and foodstuffs that are minimally processed. There are several variations to the plant-based diet, and it is easy to confuse one from the other. However, we can typically distinguish them into four main types.

Vegan – The diet consists completely of plant-based foods and excludes all kinds of animal products, making it the most restrictive among the four diets on this list. Apart from its nutritional aspect, veganism is a type of lifestyle that takes into account the ethical and environmental impacts of treating animals and animal products as a commodity.

Vegetarian – Similar to veganism, the diet is mostly plant-based with a few exceptions for some animal products that are obtained without butchering the animal. It can be further broken down into lacto, ovo and lacto-ovo. The animal products that lacto vegetarians only consume are dairy products such as milk, cheese and yogurt. Ovo vegetarians only eat eggs apart from the usual plant-based food choices. Lacto-ovo vegetarians include both eggs and dairy products in their diet.

Pescatarian – Although the diet still excludes all types of animal meats, it does allow the consumption of fish, seafood and shellfish.

Semi-vegetarian or flexitarian – The diet is the most relaxed in this list as it allows the occasional consumption of animal products. This is the plant-based diet that we will focus more on in this cookbook.

A slow cooker is a compact electrical appliance that has a pot made of ceramic or porcelain. Slow cooked meals are flavorful and easy to make, often involving only a few steps. Combining a slow cooker with a plant-based diet can guarantee that it will make your life get easier and healthier more.

Additional Useful & Interesting Information

Several studies have shown that animal agriculture or livestock farming has various environmental impacts such as increased greenhouse gas emissions, water pollution, deforestation and desertification, among others.

More and more people are taking an interest in taking a plant-based diet as internet searching for 'plant-based recipes for beginners' has increased by 85 percent.

Stuffed Peppers

No one's going to miss beef stuffed peppers when you serve this meatless appetizer. It is stuffed with a delicious combination of onion, corn, kidney beans and cooked rice.

Serving Size: 6

Preparation & Cooking Time: 8 hours and 30 minutes

Ingredients:

- ¼ cup onion, chopped
- 28 oz. canned diced tomatoes, undrained
- 10 oz. corn kernels
- 16 oz. canned kidney beans, rinsed and drained
- 1 ½ cups cooked white or brown rice
- 2 cups cheddar cheese, shredded and divided
- ¾ teaspoon chili powder
- 1 teaspoon Worcestershire sauce
- Salt and pepper to taste
- 6 green bell peppers, tops sliced off

Instructions:

Combine the onion, tomatoes, corn, kidney beans, rice and half of the cheese in a bowl.

Mix well.

Season with the chili powder, Worcestershire sauce, salt and pepper.

Stuff the bell peppers with the mixture.

Place the stuffed bell peppers in the slow cooker.

Cover the pot.

Cook on low for 8 hours.

Sprinkle the remaining cheese on top.

Cover and cook for 15 minutes or until the cheese has melted.

Nutrients per Serving:

- Calories 342
- Fat 11 g
- Saturated fat 8 g
- Carbohydrates 46 g
- Fiber 8 g
- Protein 17 g
- Cholesterol 40 mg
- Sugars 8 g
- Sodium 550 mg
- Potassium 943 mg

Artichoke & Spinach Dip

With five different types of cheese included in this creamy dip, you can expect a fusion of incredible flavors. It's no wonder that it is always among the first ones at any party. Serve the delicious dip with whole grain crackers or vegetable dippers.

Serving Size: 16

Preparation & Cooking Time: 2 hours and 30 minutes

Ingredients:

- ¼ cup red onion, chopped
- 2 cloves garlic, minced
- 6 ½ oz. jarred marinated artichoke hearts, chopped
- 12 oz. jarred roasted red bell peppers, chopped
- 8 oz. mozzarella cheese, sliced into cubes
- 6 oz. cream cheese, softened and sliced into cubes
- 1 ½ cups Asiago cheese, shredded
- 1/3 cup provolone cheese, shredded
- 1 cup feta cheese, crumbled
- 10 oz. frozen spinach, squeezed dry
- 1/3 cup fresh basil, chopped
- 2 tablespoons mayonnaise

For serving

- Crackers
- Vegetable dippers

Instructions:

Combine all of the ingredients in your slow cooker.

Cover the pot.

Cook on high for 2 hours.

Cook for 30 minutes more.

Serve with the crackers or vegetable dippers.

Nutrients per Serving:

- Calories 197
- Fat 16 g
- Saturated fat 8 g
- Carbohydrates 4 g
- Fiber 1 g
- Protein 9 g
- Cholesterol 38 mg
- Sugars 2 g
- Sodium 357 mg
- Potassium 157 mg

African Sweet Potato Stew

This is a good chance that you haven't tried making this stew at home yet. Now is the time. And once you get a taste of the creamy, savory and sweet stew, you'll be happy that you've found its recipe! Also called domadah or maafe, the stew was first introduced in Western Africa by the Bambara and Madinka people of Mali. If you like, you can also include it with chicken, lamb or beef.

Serving Size: 8

Preparation & Cooking Time: 6 hours and 20 minutes

Ingredients:

- 3 cloves garlic, sliced in half
- 1 cup cilantro leaves
- 28 oz. canned diced tomatoes
- ½ cup creamy peanut butter
- ½ teaspoon ground cinnamon
- 2 teaspoons ground cumin
- ¼ teaspoon smoked paprika
- Salt to taste
- 15 oz. chickpeas, rinsed and drained
- 3 lb. sweet potatoes, sliced into cubes
- 1 cup water
- 8 cups fresh kale, chopped

For serving

- Chopped roasted peanuts
- Fresh cilantro leaves, chopped

Instructions:

Add the garlic, cilantro, canned diced tomatoes, peanut butter, ground cinnamon, ground cumin, smoked paprika and salt to a food processor or blender.

Process until smooth.

Transfer to your slow cooker.

Add the chickpeas, sweet potatoes and water to the pot.

Cover the pot.

Cook on low for 6 hours.

In the last 30 minutes of cooking, add the kale.

Top with the peanuts and cilantro before serving.

Nutrients per Serving:

- Calories 349
- Fat 9 g
- Saturated fat 1 g
- Carbohydrates 60 g
- Fiber 11 g
- Protein 10 g
- Cholesterol 0 mg
- Sugars 23 g
- Sodium 624 mg
- Potassium 949 mg

Moroccan Chickpea Stew

Enjoy this Moroccan chickpea stew loaded with flavors that would amaze you and everyone at the dinner table. It takes 4 hours to cook, but the long wait is always worth it.

Serving Size: 6

Preparation & Cooking Time: 4 hours and 10 minutes

Ingredients:

- 1 white onion, chopped
- 3 cloves garlic, minced
- 1 teaspoon ginger, grated
- 1 red bell pepper, chopped
- 1 butternut squash, peeled and sliced into cubes
- 15 oz. canned chickpeas, rinsed and drained
- ¾ cup red lentils
- 3 cups vegetable broth
- 15 oz. canned tomato sauce
- 1 teaspoon smoked paprika
- 1 teaspoon ground cumin
- 1 teaspoon ground turmeric
- ½ teaspoon cinnamon
- Salt and pepper to taste

For serving

- Coconut yogurt
- Arugula
- Cooked quinoa

Instructions:

Put all of the ingredients in the slow cooker.

Cover the pot.

Cook on high for 4 hours.

Uncover the pot in the last 1 hour of cooking.

Serve with the coconut yogurt, arugula and cooked quinoa.

Nutrients per Serving:

- Calories 178
- Fat 3.7 g
- Saturated fat 0.5 g
- Carbohydrates 37 g
- Fiber 11 g
- Protein 8 g
- Cholesterol 0 mg
- Sugars 8 g
- Sodium 741 mg
- Potassium 968 mg

Pumpkin & Chickpea Curry

This is one curry dish that would certainly make a regular appearance at your dinner table. It's that good! If you don't have tamari, you can use soy sauce. Coconut sugar, meanwhile, can be substituted with maple syrup.

Serving Size: 6

Preparation & Cooking Time: 4 hours and 10 minutes

Ingredients:

- ½ tablespoon vegetable oil
- 1 onion, chopped
- 4 cloves garlic, minced
- 1 cup coconut milk
- 1 tablespoon coconut sugar
- 1 cup vegetable broth
- 1 ½ tablespoons tamari
- 1 tablespoon red curry paste
- 2 cups sweet potato, sliced into cubes
- 15 oz. canned chickpeas, drained and rinsed
- 2 cups pumpkin, sliced into cubes
- 1 ½ cups spinach

For serving

- Cooked rice
- Cilantro
- 4 tablespoons peanuts, crushed

Instructions:

Add the oil to a pan over medium high heat.

Cook the onion for 2 minutes.

Reduce the heat and cook the garlic for 2 minutes.

Turn off the heat.

Mix the coconut milk, coconut sugar, vegetable broth, tamari and red curry paste in a bowl.

Pour the mixture into your slow cooker.

Stir in the mixture.

Add the sweet potato, chickpeas and pumpkin to the pot.

Stir well.

Cover the pot.

Cook on high for 4 hours.

In the last 10 minutes of cooking, stir in the spinach.

Serve with the rice and top with the cilantro and peanuts.

Nutrients per Serving:

- Calories 523
- Fat 19.3 g
- Saturated Fat 10 g
- Cholesterol 0 mg
- Sodium 573 mg
- Carbohydrate 72.6 g
- Fiber 19 g
- Sugars 19.1 g
- Protein 20.2 g
- Potassium 1374 mg

Slow Cooked Pinto Beans

When it comes to easy and simple dinner ideas, this is one recipe that you can't dare miss. It only requires minimal effort to make, but the result is always impressive. Top with chopped tomatoes, cilantro and shredded cheese and serve with cubed avocado.

Serving Size: 6

Preparation & Cooking Time: 8 hours and 10 minutes

Ingredients:

- 2 cups dry pinto beans
- 2 teaspoons olive oil
- 1 yellow onion, diced
- 1 jalapeno, chopped
- 3 cloves garlic, minced
- 1 teaspoon dried oregano
- ¼ teaspoon cayenne pepper
- 1 teaspoon ground cumin
- Salt to taste
- 4 cups reduced-sodium chicken broth, divided
- 2 bay leaves
- 3 cups water

For serving

- Avocado, sliced into cubes
- Monterey Jack cheese, shredded
- Tomatoes, diced
- Red onions, diced
- Cilantro, chopped

Instructions:

Add the pinto beans to your slow cooker.

Pour the oil into a pan over medium high heat.

Cook the onion and jalapeno in the pan for 2 minutes, stirring often.

Stir in the garlic.

Cook for 1 minute.

Transfer the mixture to the slow cooker.

Stir in the rest of the ingredients.

Cover the pot.

Cook on high for 8 hours.

Discard the bay leaves.

Serve with avocado, cheese, tomatoes, red onions and cilantro.

Nutrients per Serving:

- Calories 131
- Fat 3 g
- Saturated fat 1 g
- Carbohydrates 20 g
- Fiber 6 g
- Protein 9 g
- Cholesterol 0 mg
- Sugars 1 g
- Sodium 422 mg
- Potassium 423 mg

Mixed Root Veggie Stew

This is one hearty and satisfying stew that you can make in your slow cooker. You can also make it ahead of time and freeze it until ready to serve!

Serving Size: 5

Preparation & Cooking Time: 4 hours and 30 minutes

Ingredients:

- 28 oz. canned diced tomatoes
- 4 cups rutabagas, sliced into cubes
- 4 cups butternut squash, sliced into cubes
- 2 cups carrots, chopped
- 2 cups parsnips, chopped
- 2 cups white onions, diced
- 4 cloves garlic, minced
- 1 cup vegetable stock
- 1 teaspoon ground thyme
- 2 bay leaves

For serving

- 2 tablespoons cornstarch mixed with 2 tablespoons water
- 1 tablespoon maple syrup
- Salt and pepper to taste

Instructions:

Put all of the ingredients except the serving ingredients in the slow cooker.

Stir well.

Cover the pot.

Cook on high for 4 hours.

Stir in the cornstarch mixture, maple syrup, salt and pepper.

Cook for 10 more minutes.

Nutrients per Serving:

- Calories 215
- Fat 0.8 g
- Saturated fat 0 g
- Carbohydrates 52.2 g
- Fiber 10.7 g
- Protein 4.4 g
- Cholesterol 0 mg
- Sugars 18 g
- Sodium 187 mg
- Potassium 1567 mg

Cauliflower Soup

You'll love not only the creamy and silky texture of this cauliflower soup but also the spiced chickpea topping that adds a unique flavor to the dish.

Serving Size: 4

Preparation & Cooking Time: 3 hours and 30 minutes

Ingredients:

Soup

- 1 white onion, chopped
- 4 cups cauliflower florets
- 3 cups vegetable broth
- 2 cups water
- 1 cup cashews
- ½ teaspoon salt

Topping

- 15 oz. canned chickpeas, drained
- 1 tablespoon olive oil
- ½ teaspoon ground cumin
- 1 teaspoon smoked paprika
- Salt to taste

Instructions:

Add the onion, cauliflower and cashews to the slow cooker.

Pour in the broth.

Season with the salt.

Cover the pot.

Cook on high for 3 hours.

Transfer the mixture to a blender or food processor.

Process until pureed.

Transfer to a pot.

Pour in the water.

Heat through for 10 minutes.

Preheat your oven to 400 degrees F.

Toss the chickpeas in the olive oil.

Add to a baking pan.

Season with the ground cumin, smoked paprika and salt.

Bake in the oven for 20 minutes.

Top the soup with the chickpeas and serve.

Nutrients per Serving:

- Calories 393
- Fat 21.7 g
- Saturated fat 4.1 g
- Carbohydrates 38.7 g
- Fiber 7.5 g
- Protein 15.1 g
- Cholesterol 0 mg
- Sugars 5.1 g
- Sodium 1307 mg
- Potassium 761 mg

Jackfruit

Here's an amazing way to enjoy your tacos with little or no meat. It's just as delicious! And with your slow cooker, it's also easy to prepare.

Serving Size: 4

Preparation & Cooking Time: 2 hours and 20 minutes

Ingredients:

- ¾ cup vegetable stock
- 1 onion, chopped
- 3 cloves garlic, minced
- 14 oz. canned diced tomatoes
- 1 canned chipotle in adobo sauce, minced
- 14 oz. canned jackfruit, rinsed and drained
- 1 teaspoon adobo sauce
- 1 teaspoon ground cumin
- 1 teaspoon dried oregano
- 1 bay leaf
- Salt to taste
- 4 corn tortillas
- Chopped mango
- Avocado, sliced into cubes
- Cilantro leaves
- Greek yogurt
- Sour cream
- Lime wedges

Instructions:

Add the vegetable stock to the slow cooker.

Stir in the onion, garlic, tomatoes, chipotle and jackfruit.

Add the adobo sauce.

Season with the ground cumin, dried oregano, bay leaf and salt.

Stir well.

Cover the pot.

Cook on high for 2 hours.

Transfer the jackfruit to a cutting board.

Shred with 2 forks.

Put the shredded jackfruit back to the pot.

Stir to coat with the sauce.

Top the corn tortillas with the mixture.

Sprinkle the mango, avocado and cilantro on top.

Fold the sides and roll up.

Serve with the Greek yogurt and sour cream.

Garnish with the lime wedges.

Nutrients per Serving:

- Calories 319
- Fat 2 g
- Saturated fat 0.2 g
- Carbohydrates 74 g
- Fiber 5 g
- Protein 4 g
- Cholesterol 0 mg
- Sugars 1 g
- Sodium 559 mg
- Potassium 345 mg

Vegetarian Chili

If you don't want to go completely meatless for this recipe, you can add shredded beef or pulled pork to the flavorful vegetarian chili.

Serving Size: 6

Preparation & Cooking Time: 8 hours and 30 minutes

Ingredients:

- Cooking spray
- ½ red onion, diced
- 1 green bell pepper, diced
- 1 red bell pepper, diced
- 2 stalks celery, diced
- 1 sweet potato, diced
- 1 carrot, chopped
- 8 oz. canned diced green chili
- 8 oz. canned tomato sauce
- 15 oz. canned diced tomatoes
- 15 oz. canned black beans, finely rinsed and drained
- 15 oz. canned kidney beans, finely rinsed and drained
- 15 oz. canned chickpeas, finely rinsed and drained
- 1 cup water
- 2 teaspoons garlic powder
- 2 teaspoons dried oregano
- 2 ½ tablespoons chili powder
- 1 tablespoon ground cumin
- Salt and pepper to taste

Instructions:

Spray your slow cooker with oil.

Add all of the ingredients to the pot.

Stir well.

Cover the pot.

Cook on low for 8 hours, stirring from time to time.

Nutrients per Serving:

- Calories 289
- Fat 3 g
- Saturated Fat 1 g
- Carbohydrates 53 g
- Fiber 17 g
- Protein 21 g
- Cholesterol 0 mg
- Sugar 8 g
- Sodium 769 mg
- Potassium 1007 mg

Vegetable Jambalaya

This mix of rice, vegetables and beans is a satisfying meal that even meat lovers will enjoy. Add sausage to complete the medley.

Serving Size: 8

Preparation & Cooking Time: 7 hours and 50 minutes

Ingredients:

- 1 tablespoon olive oil
- 1 white onion, chopped
- 3 cloves garlic, minced
- 2 stalks celery, diced
- 1 green bell pepper, diced
- 4 cups vegetable broth
- 1 ½ cups canned diced tomatoes
- 2 tablespoons paprika
- 2 teaspoon ground black pepper
- 2 tablespoons ground cumin
- 1 teaspoon dried oregano
- 1 teaspoon dried thyme
- 2 tablespoons hot pepper sauce
- 2 cups long grain brown rice
- 1 ¾ cups cooked kidney beans
- 2 cups sausage, sliced
- 2 scallions, chopped

Instructions:

Add the oil, white onion, garlic, celery, bell pepper, vegetable broth, tomatoes, paprika, black pepper, ground cumin, dried oregano, dried thyme and hot pepper sauce to your slow cooker.

Cover the pot.

Cook on low for 6 hours, stirring from time to time.

Add the brown rice to the pot.

Increase heat to high.

Stir and cook for 1 hour and 30 minutes, stirring from time to time.

Stir in the sausage and beans.

Cook for 5 minutes.

Top with the scallions before serving.

Nutrients per Serving:

- Calories 514
- Fat 7.7 g
- Saturated Fat 1.5 g
- Carbohydrate 90.6 g
- Fiber 13.2 g
- Protein 22.8 g
- Cholesterol 4 mg
- Sugars 5.1 g
- Sodium 564 mg
- Potassium 1359 mg

Apple Butter

Once you learn how easy it is to make your own apple butter, you're never going to buy jarred apple butter ever again! Apple butter is made by slow cooking slices of apples with cinnamon and nutmeg until the apples caramelize and turn into deep brown color. Use the butter to top your oatmeal or pancakes, or serve with toasted bread slices. It can be stored in the refrigerator for up to 3 weeks.

Serving Size: 8

Preparation & Cooking Time: 6 hours and 10 minutes

Ingredients:

- 8 apples, cored and sliced
- 2 teaspoons cinnamon
- ½ teaspoon nutmeg

Instructions:

Add the apples to your slow cooker.

Sprinkle with the cinnamon and nutmeg.

Cover the pot.

Cook low for 6 hours.

Let cool before serving or storing in an airtight container.

Nutrients per Serving:

- Calories 118
- Fat 0.5 g
- Saturated Fat 0 g
- Carbohydrate 31.3 g
- Fiber 5.7 g
- Protein 0.6 g
- Cholesterol 0 mg
- Sugars 23.3 g
- Sodium 2 mg
- Potassium 242 mg

Eggplant Lasagna

Want something different to bring to your next potluck? How about noodle-free lasagna? Instead of noodles, we make use of eggplant and zucchini slices and layer them with the same ingredients you love in your lasagna. The result is a cheesy low carb dish that comes out of the slow cooker after a few hours.

Serving Size: 6

Preparation & Cooking Time: 3 hours and 15 minutes

Ingredients:

- 1 eggplant, sliced
- 2 zucchinis, sliced
- Salt to taste
- 16 oz. tomato pasta sauce
- 2 eggs, beaten
- 16 oz. cottage cheese
- 1 red onion, chopped
- 1 red bell pepper, chopped
- ¼ cup lean ground beef, cooked
- 8 oz. mozzarella cheese

For serving

- Chopped fresh basil
- Grated Parmesan cheese

Instructions:

Arrange the eggplant and zucchini slices on a large plate.

Sprinkle both sides with salt.

Let sit for 15 minutes.

Dry with paper towels.

Spread the tomato sauce on the bottom of the slow cooker.

In a bowl, mix the eggs and cottage cheese.

Put the eggplant and zucchini slices on top of the tomato sauce.

Spread with another layer of the tomato sauce.

Top with the onion, bell pepper, beef and cheese.

Spread the cream cheese mixture on top.

Top with another layer of eggplant and zucchini.

Repeat the layers.

On the topmost layer, sprinkle the mozzarella cheese.

Cover the pot.

Cook on high for 3 hours.

Sprinkle with the basil and Parmesan cheese before serving.

Nutrients per Serving:

- Calories 519
- Fat 19.1 g
- Saturated Fat 8.7 g
- Carbohydrate 16.7 g
- Fiber 4.7 g
- Protein 68.6 g
- Cholesterol 207 mg
- Sugars 6.9 g
- Sodium 837 mg
- Potassium 1074 mg

Slow Cooked Black Beans

One of the best ways to cook black beans is using your slow cooker. Slow cooking the beans doesn't only make them tender enough to enjoy, but if mixed with the right spices, it also infuses them with delightful flavors.

Serving Size: 6

Preparation & Cooking Time: 8 hours and 10 minutes

Ingredients:

- 1 onion, chopped
- 4 cloves garlic, sliced
- 2 ½ cups dried black beans
- 1 teaspoon ground coriander
- 1 tablespoon ground cumin
- 1 teaspoon dried mint leaves
- 2 teaspoons red pepper flakes
- 1 bay leaf
- 1 tablespoon lime juice
- 3 ½ cups vegetable broth

Instructions:

Add all of the ingredients to your slow cooker.

Cover the pot.

Cook on low for 8 hours.

Nutrients per Serving:

- Calories 316
- Fat 2.3 g
- Saturated Fat 0.6 g
- Carbohydrate 54.8 g
- Fiber 13.1 g
- Protein 20.9 g
- Cholesterol 0 mg
- Sugars 3.1 g
- Sodium 452 mg
- Potassium 1395 mg

Tofu Tikka Masala

This is a meat-free version of the famous Indian dish that would satisfy your cravings for a dish with strong flavors and aroma.

Serving Size: 4

Preparation & Cooking Time: 6 hours and 15 minutes

Ingredients:

Spice mixture

- ½ teaspoon ground turmeric
- 2 tablespoons paprika
- 1 tablespoon garam masala
- 1 teaspoon ground coriander
- ½ teaspoon cayenne pepper
- Salt and pepper to taste

Tikka masala

- 1 pack tofu, sliced into cubes
- 1 tablespoon coconut oil
- 1 teaspoon cumin seeds
- 1 yellow onion, chopped
- 4 cloves garlic, minced
- 2 green chili peppers, chopped
- 1 tablespoon ginger, minced
- 1 red bell pepper, sliced
- 6 tablespoons tomato paste
- 3 tablespoons nutritional yeast
- 2 cups cherry tomatoes, sliced
- 1 teaspoon coconut sugar
- 2 tablespoons white wine vinegar
- 1 ¾ cups coconut milk
- Salt to taste

For serving

- Lemon juice
- Chopped fresh cilantro

Instructions:

Combine the spice mixture ingredients in a bowl and set aside.

Pour the coconut oil into a pan over medium heat.

Cook the onion for 5 minutes, stirring often.

Season with the salt.

Stir in the cumin seeds.

Cook while stirring for 1 minute.

Add the garlic, chili pepper and ginger.

Cook for another 1 minute.

Add the spice mixture to the pan.

Cook for 45 seconds.

Stir in the bell pepper, tomato paste and nutritional yeast.

Cook for 2 minutes, stirring often.

Add the tomatoes and cook for 3 minutes.

Turn off the heat.

Add the tofu to your slow cooker.

Add the rest of the ingredients.

Stir in the tomato mixture from the pan.

Stir well.

Cover the pot.

Cook on low for 6 hours.

Drizzle with the lemon juice.

Garnish with the cilantro before serving.

Nutrients per Serving:

- Calories 383
- Fat 26 g
- Saturated Fat 18 g
- Carbohydrates 23 g
- Fiber 7 g
- Protein 18 g
- Cholesterol 0 mg
- Sugar 10 g
- Sodium 74 mg
- Potassium 1038 mg

Butternut Squash Soup

Butternut squash is a delicious source of vitamin A, vitamin C, vitamin B and potassium. Take advantage of the nutrient-dense vegetable by cooking it in your slow cooker and pureeing it to serve as a soup. It's a good idea to make a big batch of the soup and store it in the freezer for up to 3 months, so you have a ready-to-heat soup anytime you're craving the dish.

Serving Size: 8

Preparation & Cooking Time: 8 hours and 10 minutes

Ingredients:

- 2 cups white onion, chopped
- 4 cloves garlic, minced
- 1 cup carrot, chopped
- 1 butternut squash, sliced into cubes
- ½ teaspoon cinnamon
- 6 cups vegetable broth
- Pinch ground nutmeg
- Pepper to taste
- ½ cup coconut milk

Instructions:

Put all of the ingredients except the coconut milk to your slow cooker.

Cover the pot.

Cook on low for 8 hours.

Transfer the mixture to your blender or food processor.

Process until pureed.

Stir in the coconut milk.

Heat through for 5 minutes before serving.

Nutrients per Serving:

- Calories 174
- Fat 6.4 g
- Saturated Fat 4.7 g
- Carbohydrate 24.6 g
- Fiber 4.7 g
- Protein 7.4 g
- Cholesterol 0 mg
- Sugars 7 g
- Sodium 786 mg
- Potassium 876 mg

Tortilla Lasagna

In one of the previous recipes, we learned how to make lasagna swapping noodles with eggplant and zucchini slices. This time, we make lasagna with tortillas and layer it with vegetables.

Serving Size: 8

Preparation & Cooking Time: 3 hours and 20 minutes

Ingredients:

- Cooking spray
- 1 cup salsa
- 6 oz. tomato paste
- 14 ½ oz. canned diced tomatoes with garlic and herbs
- 15 oz. canned black beans, rinsed and drained
- 15 ½ oz. hominy, rinsed and drained
- ½ teaspoon ground cumin
- 3 flour tortillas
- 2 cups Monterey Jack cheese, shredded
- ¼ cup ripe olives, sliced

Instructions:

Spray your slow cooker with oil.

In a bowl, mix the salsa, tomato paste and tomatoes.

Stir in the beans, hominy and cumin.

Add one tortilla inside the slow cooker.

Top with the tomato mixture and then with the cheese.

Repeat the layers.

Top with the olives.

Cover the pot.

Cook on low for 3 hours.

Let sit for 5 minutes before transferring to a plate and serving.

Nutrients per Serving:

- Calories 335
- Fat 12 g
- Saturated fat 6 g
- Carbohydrates 41 g
- Fiber 8 g
- Protein 15 g
- Cholesterol 25 mg
- Sugars 6 g
- Sodium 1166 mg
- Potassium 778 mg

Vegetable Buffalo Dip

This appetizer is so good you probably won't miss the meal! Here's how you can make the vegetarian version of a buffalo dip using your slow cooker.

Serving Size: 6

Preparation & Cooking Time: 1 hour and 50 minutes

Ingredients:

- 1 packet ranch salad dressing mix
- 8 oz. cream cheese
- 1 cup sour cream
- 2 cups sharp cheddar cheese, shredded
- 1 cup Buffalo wing sauce
- 8 oz. fresh mushrooms, chopped
- 15 oz. canned black beans, rinsed and drained

For serving

- Chopped green onions
- Vegetable sticks
- Tortilla chips

Instructions:

Add the ranch dressing, cream cheese and sour cream to a bowl.

Mix well.

Stir in the cheddar cheese, Buffalo wing sauce, mushrooms and black beans.

Transfer the mixture to your slow cooker.

Cover the pot.

Cook on high for 1 hour and 30 minutes.

Sprinkle the dip with the green onion.

Serve with the vegetable sticks and tortilla chips.

Nutrients per Serving:

- Calories 113
- Fat 8 g
- Saturated fat 5 g
- Carbohydrates 5 g
- Fiber 1 g
- Protein 4 g
- Cholesterol 21 mg
- Sugars 1 g
- Sodium 526 mg
- Potassium 667 mg

Spiced Acorn Squashes

Cook spiced acorn squashes in your slow cooker for a healthy snack that supplies you with much-needed nutrients.

Serving Size: 4

Preparation & Cooking Time: 3 hours and 40 minutes

Ingredients:

- 1 teaspoon ground cinnamon
- ¾ cup brown sugar
- 1 teaspoon ground nutmeg
- 2 acorn squashes, sliced in half and seeded
- ¾ cup raisins
- 4 tablespoons butter
- ½ cup water

Instructions:

Combine the ground cinnamon, brown sugar and ground nutmeg.

Top the acorn squashes with the mixture.

Sprinkle the raisins on top.

Spoon the butter on top of the squashes.

Wrap each half with foil.

Pour the water into your slow cooker.

Place the wrapped squashes inside the pot.

Cover the pot.

Cook on high for 3 hours and 30 minutes.

Nutrients per Serving:

- Calories 433
- Fat 12 g
- Saturated fat 7 g
- Carbohydrates 86 g
- Fiber 5 g
- Protein 3 g
- Cholesterol 31 mg
- Sugars 63 g
- Sodium 142 mg
- Potassium 895 mg

Slow Cooked Broccoli

This slow cooked broccoli dish easily becomes a family favorite. Don't make the mistake of thinking it's just a side dish. It's delicious enough to be the center of attention during dinnertime.

Serving Size: 10

Preparation & Cooking Time: 3 hours and 10 minutes

Ingredients:

- 1 ½ cups sharp cheddar cheese, shredded and divided
- ¼ cup onion, chopped
- 10 ¾ oz. cream of celery soup
- ½ teaspoon Worcestershire sauce
- 6 cups broccoli florets
- Pepper to taste
- 25 butter crackers, crushed
- 2 tablespoons butter

Instructions:

Add 1 cup of the cheese to a bowl.

Stir in the onion, cream of celery soup, Worcestershire sauce, broccoli florets and pepper.

Transfer the mixture to your slow cooker.

Sprinkle the crackers on top.

Spread the butter on top of the crackers.

Cover the pot.

Cook on high for 2 hours and 30 minutes.

Sprinkle the remaining cheese on top.

Cook for 10 more minutes.

Nutrients per Serving:

- Calories 159
- Fat 11 g
- Saturated fat 6 g
- Carbohydrates 11 g
- Fiber 1 g
- Protein 6 g
- Cholesterol 25 mg
- Sugars 2 g
- Sodium 431 mg
- Potassium 690 mg

Mushroom Marsala

This is a delicious fusion of the 2 popular dishes: mushroom and barley soup and chicken Marsala. It's delicious, filling and easy to prepare.

Serving Size: 6

Preparation & Cooking Time: 4 hours and 50 minutes

Ingredients:

- 3 tablespoons olive oil
- 1 cup shallots, chopped
- ½ teaspoon fresh thyme, minced
- 1 ½ lb. Portobello mushrooms, sliced
- ¾ cup Marsala wine, divided
- 2 tablespoons all-purpose flour
- 3 tablespoons low-fat sour cream
- 1 ½ teaspoons lemon zest, grated
- Salt to taste
- ¼ cup parsley, minced
- ¼ cup goat cheese, crumbled
- 2 ½ cups barley, cooked

Instructions:

Combine the olive oil, shallots, thyme and mushrooms.

Pour in ¼ cup of the Marsala wine.

Stir well.

Cover the pot.

Cook on low for 4 hours.

Stir in the flour, sour cream and lemon zest.

Season with the salt.

Pour in the remaining wine.

Cover and cook for 15 minutes.

Top with the parsley and goat cheese.

Serve with the barley on the side.

Nutrients per Serving:

- Calories 235
- Fat 9 g
- Saturated fat 2 g
- Carbohydrates 31 g
- Fiber 5 g
- Protein 7 g
- Cholesterol 7 mg
- Sugars 6 g
- Sodium 139 mg
- Potassium 294 mg

Slow Cooker Baked Potatoes

Have extra potatoes you don't know what to do with? Here's a recipe that lets you cook baked potatoes in the slow cooker. It's just as creamy, delicious and filling as you'd expect in your baked potatoes.

Serving Size: 6

Preparation & Cooking Time: 8 hours and 10 minutes

Ingredients:

- 6 potatoes
- 3 cloves garlic, minced
- 3 tablespoons butter, softened
- 1 cup water
- Salt and pepper to taste

Toppings

- Sour cream
- Butter
- Bacon, cooked crisp and crumbled
- Cheddar cheese, shredded
- Chopped chives
- Guacamole

Instructions:

Pierce the potatoes with a fork.

In a bowl, mix the garlic and butter.

Rub the potatoes with the mixture.

Wrap the potatoes with foil.

Pour the water into your slow cooker.

Add the wrapped potatoes.

Cover the pot.

Cook on low for 8 hours.

Season with the salt and pepper.

Serve with the toppings.

Nutrients per Serving:

- Calories 217
- Fat 6 g
- Saturated fat 4 g
- Carbohydrates 38 g
- Fiber 5 g
- Protein 5 g
- Cholesterol 15 mg
- Sugars 2 g
- Sodium 59 mg
- Potassium 875 mg

Sweet Potato Stew with Lentils

Once you get started cooking this stew in your slow cooker, it's hard not to be enticed by its enticing aroma. After long hours of waiting, you'll be happy that it's finally ready!

Serving Size: 6

Preparation & Cooking Time: 5 hours and 20 minutes

Ingredients:

- 32 oz. vegetable broth
- 1 onion, chopped
- 4 cloves garlic, minced
- 1 ½ cups dried lentils, rinsed
- 1 ¼ lb. sweet potatoes, sliced into cubes
- 3 carrots, sliced into cubes
- ¼ teaspoon cayenne pepper
- ¼ teaspoon ground ginger
- ¼ cup fresh cilantro, minced

Instructions:

Add all of the ingredients except the cilantro to the slow cooker.

Cover the pot.

Cook on low for 5 hours.

Stir in the cilantro before serving.

Nutrients per Serving:

- Calories 290
- Fat 1 g
- Saturated fat 0 g
- Carbohydrates 58 g
- Fiber 15 g
- Protein 15 g
- Cholesterol 0 mg
- Sugars 16 g
- Sodium 662 mg
- Potassium 1498 mg

Chickpea Tagine

Tagine is a Moroccan dish that's hard not to fall in love with. In this recipe, we make a veggie-based version of the dish.

Serving Size: 12

Preparation & Cooking Time: 4 hours and 30 minutes

Ingredients:

- 1 butternut squash, sliced into cubes
- 1 onion, chopped
- 1 sweet red pepper, chopped
- 2 zucchinis, sliced
- 12 dried apricots, sliced in half
- 15 oz. chickpeas, rinsed and drained
- 2 tablespoons olive oil
- 2 cloves garlic, minced
- Salt and pepper to taste
- 1 teaspoon ground ginger
- 2 teaspoons paprika
- ¼ teaspoon ground cinnamon
- 1 teaspoon ground cumin
- 15 oz. canned crushed tomatoes
- 2 teaspoons chili paste
- 2 teaspoons honey
- ¼ cup fresh mint leaves, chopped
- Greek yogurt

For serving

- Honey
- Olive oil
- Fresh mint leaves

Instructions:

Combine the butternut squash, onion, sweet red pepper, zucchinis, dried apricots and chickpeas in your slow cooker.

Add the oil to a pan over medium heat.

Cook the garlic and ginger for 1 minute, stirring often.

Season with the salt, pepper, paprika, ground cinnamon and ground cumin.

Stir in the honey, tomatoes and chili paste.

Pour the mixture into the pot.

Cover the pot.

Cook on low for 5 hours.

Drizzle with the honey and olive oil.

Garnish with the fresh mint leaves.

Nutrients per Serving:

- Calories 127
- Fat 3 g
- Saturated fat 0 g
- Carbohydrates 23 g
- Fiber 6 g
- Protein 4 g
- Cholesterol 0 mg
- Sugars 9 g
- Sodium 224 mg
- Potassium 780 mg

Sweet & Savory Beans

Wondering what to bring to your next potluck? Here's a no-fail idea that won't cost you too much and doesn't take a lot of effort to make.

Serving Size: 16

Preparation & Cooking Time: 5 hours and 10 minutes

Ingredients:

- 1 onion, chopped
- 1 sweet red pepper, chopped
- 1 green pepper, chopped
- 1 ½ cups ketchup
- ½ cup brown sugar
- ½ cup water
- 1 teaspoon ground mustard
- 2 teaspoons cider vinegar
- 2 bay leaves
- Pinch pepper
- 15 ½ oz. great northern beans, rinsed and drained
- 16 oz. kidney beans, rinsed and drained
- 15 oz. black beans, rinsed and drained
- 15 ¼ oz. lima beans
- 15 ½ oz. black eyed peas, rinsed and drained
- ½ cup crumbled turkey bacon or Italian sausage

Instructions:

Add the onion, sweet red pepper, green pepper, ketchup, brown sugar, water, ground mustard, cider vinegar, bay leaves and pepper to your slow cooker.

Mix well.

Stir in the remaining ingredients.

Cover the pot.

Cook on low for 5 hours.

Remove the bay leaves before serving.

Nutrients per Serving:

- Calories 166
- Fat 0 g
- Saturated fat 0 g
- Carbohydrates 34 g
- Fiber 7 g
- Protein 6 g
- Cholesterol 0 mg
- Sugars 15 g
- Sodium 528 mg
- Potassium 1418 mg

Butternut Squash & Whole Grains

Whole grain pilaf, butternut squash and fresh thyme come together to create this fantastic dish that even meat lovers would appreciate.

Serving Size: 12

Preparation & Cooking Time: 4 hours and 15 minutes

Ingredients:

- ½ cup water
- 14 ½ oz. vegetable broth
- 1 onion, minced
- 3 cloves garlic, minced
- 1 cup whole grain red and brown rice
- 3 lb. butternut squash, sliced into cubes
- 2 teaspoons fresh thyme, sliced
- Salt and pepper to taste
- 6 oz. baby spinach

Instructions:

Pour the water and vegetable broth to your slow cooker. Stir.

Add the onion, garlic, rice blend, butternut squash and fresh thyme.

Season with the salt and pepper.

Cover the pot.

Cook on low for4 hours.

In the last 10 minutes of cooking, add the spinach.

Nutrients per Serving:

- Calories 97
- Fat 1 g
- Saturated fat 0 g
- Carbohydrates 22 g
- Fiber 4 g
- Protein 3 g
- Cholesterol 0 mg
- Sugars 3 g
- Sodium 252 mg
- Potassium 526 mg

Enchilada Pie

This enchilada pie gives you layer after layer of flavor, nutrients and satisfaction. It's an impressive dish that surprisingly doesn't require complicated preparations.

Serving Size: 8

Preparation & Cooking Time: 4 hours and 40 minutes

Ingredients:

- Cooking spray
- 2 teaspoons vegetable oil
- 1 cup onion, chopped
- ½ cup green bell pepper, chopped
- 12 oz. ground chicken or ground lean beef
- 10 oz. canned tomatoes with green chili
- 15 oz. black beans, rinsed and drained
- 16 oz. kidney beans, rinsed and drained
- ½ cup water
- ½ teaspoon ground cumin
- 1 ½ teaspoons chili powder
- Pepper to taste
- 6 whole wheat tortillas
- 2 cups cheddar cheese, shredded

Toppings

- Sour cream
- Fresh Cilantro, chopped
- Salsa
- Lime wedges

Instructions:

Line the bottom part of your slow cooker with foil.

Spray the foil with oil.

Add the vegetable oil to a pan over medium heat.

Cook the onion, green bell pepper and ground meat for 5 to 7 minutes, stirring often.

Stir in the canned tomatoes, black beans and kidney beans.

Pour in the water.

Season with the ground cumin, chili powder and pepper.

Bring to a boil.

Reduce heat and simmer for 10 minutes.

Spread the mixture in the slow cooker.

Top with 1 tortilla and with the cheese.

Repeat the layers until all of the ingredients have been used.

Cover the pot.

Cook on low for 4 hours.

Serve with the toppings.

Nutrients per Serving:

- Calories 367
- Fat 11 g
- Saturated fat 4 g
- Carbohydrates 41 g
- Fiber 9 g
- Protein 25 g
- Cholesterol 20 mg
- Sugars 5 g
- Sodium 818 mg
- Potassium 887.5 mg

Minestrone

You'll love the fresh and delicious flavors of this colorful soup dish that you'll surely find comforting as well. You can also use baby spinach instead of Swiss chard.

Serving Size: 10

Preparation & Cooking Time: 6 hours and 20 minutes

Ingredients:

- 2 tablespoons olive oil
- 1 red onion, minced
- ½ lb. Swiss chard
- 29 oz. canned roasted diced tomatoes, undrained
- 6 cups vegetable broth
- 2 cloves garlic, minced
- 1 yellow pepper, chopped
- 15 oz. canned chickpeas, rinsed and drained
- 16 oz. canned kidney beans, rinsed and drained
- 1 zucchini, sliced
- 1 carrot, chopped
- 1 ½ cups pasta shells
- ¼ cup pesto

Toppings

- Chopped fresh basil
- Parmesan cheese, shredded
- Red pepper flakes
- Pesto

Instructions:

Add the oil to a pan over medium heat.

Cook the onion and Swiss chard for 3 minutes.

Transfer the mixture to your slow cooker.

Pour in the tomatoes and broth.

Add the garlic, yellow pepper, chickpeas, kidney beans, zucchini and carrot.

Cover the pot.

Cook on low for 6 hours.

Add the pasta shells.

Cook for 20 minutes.

Stir in the pesto.

Top with the fresh basil, Parmesan cheese, red pepper flakes and additional pesto before serving.

Nutrients per Serving:

- Calories 231
- Fat 7 g
- Saturated fat 1 g
- Carbohydrates 34 g
- Fiber 6 g
- Protein 9 g
- Cholesterol 2 mg
- Sugars 7 g
- Sodium 1015 mg
- Potassium 663.5 mg

Spicy Ham, Lentil & Chickpea Stew

Want to impress a crowd? Here's a stress-free way to do it—serve them with a pot of ham, lentil and chickpea stew that's loaded with both flavor and nutrients.

Serving Size: 8

Preparation & Cooking Time: 8 hours and 30 minutes

Ingredients:

- 2 teaspoons olive oil
- 1 onion, sliced thinly
- ½ teaspoon red pepper flakes
- 1 teaspoon dried oregano
- 2 ¼ oz. black olives, sliced
- 1 cup dried lentils, rinsed
- 30 oz. chickpeas, rinsed and drained
- 2 slices ham, sliced into smaller cubes
- 3 teaspoons smoked paprika
- 32 oz. tomato sauce
- 4 cups vegetable broth
- 4 cups baby spinach
- ¾ cup yogurt

Instructions:

Add the oil to a pan over medium high heat.

Cook the onion, red pepper flakes and oregano for 8 minutes, stirring often.

Transfer the mixture to your slow cooker.

Stir in the black olives, dried lentils, chickpeas, ham and paprika.

Pour in the tomato sauce and vegetable broth.

Cover the pot.

Cook on low for 8 hours.

In the last 10 minutes of cooking, stir in the spinach.

Top with the yogurt before serving.

Nutrients per Serving:

- Calories 266
- Fat 4 g
- Saturated fat 0 g
- Carbohydrates 45 g
- Fiber 10 g
- Protein 14 g
- Cholesterol 0 mg
- Sugars 11 g
- Sodium 712 mg
- Potassium 781 mg

Butternut Squash & Cinnamon Soup

This golden and silky soup is a combination of tangy, sweet and savory flavors.

Serving Size: 14

Preparation & Cooking Time: 6 hours and 30 minutes

Ingredients:

- 2 tablespoons butter
- 1 onion, minced
- 1 butternut squash, sliced into cubes
- 1 clove garlic, minced
- 1 tablespoon ginger, minced
- 1 tablespoon brown sugar
- 14 ½ oz. vegetable broth
- 1 stick cinnamon
- 8 oz. cream cheese, sliced into cubes

Topping

- Black pepper to taste
- Crystallized ginger, chopped

Instructions:

Add the butter to a pan over medium heat.

Cook the onion for 2 minutes, stirring often.

Transfer the onion to your slow cooker.

Stir in the squash.

In a bowl, mix the garlic, ginger, brown sugar, vegetable broth and cinnamon.

Pour the mixture into the pot.

Cover the pot.

Cook on low for 6 hours.

Remove the cinnamon stick.

Let cool.

Transfer the soup to a blender.

Process the soup until smooth.

Put the mixture back to the pot.

Stir in the cream cheese.

Cover the pot.

Cook until the cheese has melted.

Top with the pepper and crystallized ginger.

Nutrients per Serving:

- Calories 135
- Fat 7 g
- Saturated fat 5 g
- Carbohydrates 17 g
- Fiber 4 g
- Protein 2 g
- Cholesterol 22 mg
- Sugars 5 g
- Sodium 483 mg
- Potassium 204 mg

Feta Cheese Dip

This is a mix of your favorites: feta cheese, cream cheese, sweet peppers, potatoes and basil. It's great to serve during parties. Serve with tortilla chips or crusty bread slices.

Serving Size: 2

Preparation & Cooking Time: 6 hours and 30 minutes

Ingredients:

- 2 cups potatoes, sliced into cubes
- ½ cup sweet red pepper, chopped
- 3 tablespoons fresh basil, minced
- ¼ cup water
- 8 oz. cream cheese
- 1 ½ cups feta cheese, crumbled

For serving

- Tortilla chips
- French bread baguette, sliced

Instructions:

Add the potatoes, sweet red pepper and basil to your slow cooker.

Cover the pot.

Cook on low for 6 hours or until tender.

Transfer the mixture to a blender or food processor.

Process until pureed.

Stir in the remaining ingredients.

Serve with the tortilla chips or bread.

Nutrients per Serving:

- Calories 155
- Fat 13 g
- Saturated fat 8 g
- Carbohydrates 2 g
- Fiber 1 g
- Protein 5 g
- Cholesterol 42 mg
- Sugars 1 g
- Sodium 362 mg
- Potassium 551 mg

Italian Squash

Here's a simple way to prepare your spaghetti squash—stuff it with a mix of tomatoes, mushrooms, cheese and herbs, and cook in the slow cooker.

Serving Size: 4

Preparation & Cooking Time: 8 hours and 30 minutes

Ingredients:

- 1 cup mushrooms, sliced
- 14 oz. canned diced tomatoes
- ½ teaspoon dried oregano
- Salt and pepper to taste
- 1 spaghetti squash, sliced in half and seeded
- ¾ cup mozzarella cheese, shredded

Instructions:

In a bowl, mix the mushrooms, tomatoes, dried oregano, salt and pepper in a bowl.

Stuff the squash with the mixture.

Add the squash to your slow cooker.

Cover the pot.

Cook on low for 8 hours.

Sprinkle with the mozzarella cheese.

Cook for 15 more minutes.

Let cool, slice and serve.

Nutrients per Serving:

- Calories 195
- Fat 6 g
- Saturated fat 3 g
- Carbohydrates 31 g
- Fiber 7 g
- Protein 9 g
- Cholesterol 14 mg
- Sugars 4 g
- Sodium 661 mg
- Potassium 819 mg

Vegetables & Beans

You'd want to include this veggie and bean dish in your weekly menu rotation more often. Not only is it easy to make in your slow cooker but also packed with nutritional goodness.

Serving Size: 8

Preparation & Cooking Time: 4 hours and 15 minutes

Ingredients:

- 1 cup vegetable broth
- 6 cloves garlic, minced
- 2 cups carrots, chopped
- 62 oz. great northern beans, rinsed and drained
- 2 teaspoons ground cumin
- Pinch chili powder
- Salt to taste
- 1 cup sun-dried tomatoes, chopped
- 4 cups fresh baby spinach, chopped
- ¼ cup fresh parsley, chopped
- ¼ cup fresh cilantro, minced

Instructions:

Pour the vegetable broth into your slow cooker.

Stir in the garlic, carrots and great northern beans.

Season with the ground cumin, chili powder and salt.

Cover the pot.

Cook on low for 4 hours.

In the last 10 minutes of cooking, stir in the tomatoes and spinach.

Add the parsley and cilantro before serving.

Nutrients per Serving:

- Calories 229
- Fat 3 g
- Saturated fat 0 g
- Carbohydrates 40 g
- Fiber 13 g
- Protein 12 g
- Cholesterol 0 mg
- Sugars 2 g
- Sodium 672 mg
- Potassium 1106 mg

Cheesy Spinach

Even those who don't like spinach will fall in love with these nutritious leafy greens once they get a taste of the awesome dish. It is so good; you shouldn't expect any leftovers of it!

Serving Size: 8

Preparation & Cooking Time: 5 hours and 20 minutes

Ingredients:

- 3 eggs, beaten
- 20 oz. spinach, chopped
- 1 ½ cups processed cheese, sliced into cubes
- 2 cups cottage cheese
- ¼ cup all-purpose flour
- ¼ cup butter, sliced into cubes
- Salt to taste

Instructions:

Mix all of the ingredients in your slow cooker.

Cover the pot.

Cook on high for 1 hour.

Reduce heat.

Cook on low for 4 hours.

Nutrients per Serving:

- Calories 230
- Fat 15 g
- Saturated fat 9 g
- Carbohydrates 9 g
- Fiber 1 g
- Protein 14 g
- Cholesterol 121 mg
- Sugars 4 g
- Sodium 855 mg
- Potassium 539 mg

Sweet Potatoes with Walnuts & Maple

Sweet potatoes made more flavorful by walnuts, dried cherries and maple—this dish is sure to satisfy. Everyone is likely to get a second serving of it.

Serving Size: 12

Preparation & Cooking Time: 5 hours and 20 minutes

Ingredients:

- 8 sweet potatoes, sliced into cubes
- ½ cup brown sugar
- ¼ cup apple cider
- ¾ cup walnuts, chopped and divided
- ½ cup maple syrup
- ½ cup dried cherries, chopped
- Salt to taste

Instructions:

Toss all of the ingredients into your slow cooker.

Seal the pot.

Cook on low for 5 hours.

Nutrients per Serving:

- Calories 298
- Fat 5 g
- Saturated fat 0 g
- Carbohydrates 62 g
- Fiber 5 g
- Protein 4 g
- Cholesterol 0 mg
- Sugars 37 g
- Sodium 70 mg
- Potassium 694 mg

Potato Soup

You can't get enough of this creamy and savory potato soup dish that's delightful in every spoonful. Include it with some carrots to add more color.

Serving Size: 10

Preparation & Cooking Time: 8 hours and 45 minutes

Ingredients:

- 5 cups water
- 2 cups onions, chopped
- ½ cup celery, chopped
- ½ cup carrots, sliced thinly
- 6 cups potatoes, sliced into cubes
- 4 teaspoons chicken bouillon granules
- Salt and pepper to taste
- ¼ cup butter, sliced into cubes
- 12 oz. canned evaporated milk
- 3 tablespoons fresh parsley, minced
- Chopped chives

Instructions:

Pour the water into your slow cooker.

Add the onions, celery, carrots and potatoes. Stir well.

Season with the chicken bouillon granules, salt and pepper.

Stir in the butter.

Cover the pot.

Cook on low for 8 hours.

Stir in the milk.

Sprinkle with the parsley.

Cover the pot.

Cook for 30 minutes more.

Top with the chives before serving.

Nutrients per Serving:

- Calories 190
- Saturated fat 0 g
- Fat 7 g
- Carbohydrates 26 g
- Fiber 0 g
- Protein 5 g
- Cholesterol 12 mg
- Sugars 0 g
- Sodium 827 mg
- Potassium 542 mg

Cheesy Creamed Corn

Cheesy creamed corn is one of the simplest and most hassle-free dishes that you can cook in your slow cooker. And you'll only need a bunch of ingredients!

Serving Size: 8

Preparation & Cooking Time: 3 hours and 10 minutes

Ingredients:

- ¼ cup butter, melted
- 28 oz. corn kernels
- ¾ cup cheddar cheese, shredded
- 8 oz. cream cheese, sliced into cubes
- ¼ cup heavy whipping cream
- Salt and pepper to taste

Instructions:

Mix all of the ingredients in your slow cooker.

Cover the pot.

Cook on low for 3 hours.

Stir and serve.

Nutrients per Serving:

- Calories 272
- Fat 20 g
- Saturated fat 12 g
- Carbohydrates 20 g
- Fiber 2 g
- Protein 7 g
- Cholesterol 56 mg
- Sugars 3 g
- Sodium 317 mg
- Potassium 501.6 mg

Stuffed Onions

Cooking sweet onions in broth and stuffing them with a combination of three types of cheese gives you a delectable appetizer that everyone would love.

Serving Size: 8

Preparation & Cooking Time: 4 hours and 30 minutes

Ingredients:

- 4 large sweet onions, peeled and tops sliced off
- ¾ cup blue cheese, crumbled
- ¾ cup goat cheese, crumbled
- 1 teaspoon fresh thyme, minced
- 2 cups vegetable broth
- 1 tablespoon olive oil
- ¼ cup Romano cheese, grated
- Salt and pepper to taste
- Fresh thyme leaves, chopped

Instructions:

Scoop out the center of the onions.

Chop the center part.

In a bowl, mix the blue cheese, goat cheese and thyme.

Stuff the onions with the mixture.

Pour the vegetable broth into your slow cooker.

Add the onions to the pot.

Drizzle with the olive oil.

Sprinkle with the Romano cheese, salt and pepper.

Cover the pot.

Cook on low for 4 hours.

Garnish with the thyme leaves before serving.

Nutrients per Serving:

- Calories 137
- Fat 9 g
- Saturated fat 5 g
- Carbohydrates 8 g
- Fiber 2 g
- Protein 7 g
- Cholesterol 23 mg
- Sugars 3 g
- Sodium 471 mg
- Potassium 195 mg

Barbecue & Salsa Beans

Season your beans with a barbecue sauce and salsa for an incredible snack that lets you stay full for almost the whole day.

Serving Size: 16

Preparation & Cooking Time: 2 hours and 10 minutes

Ingredients:

- 15 oz. black beans, rinsed and drained
- 15 ½ oz. great northern beans, rinsed and drained
- 30 oz. butter beans, rinsed and drained
- 2 ¼ cups barbecue sauce
- 2 ¼ cups salsa
- ¾ cup brown sugar
- 1 teaspoon hot pepper sauce

Instructions:

Add all of the ingredients to your slow cooker.

Mix well.

Cover the pot.

Cook on low for 2 hours.

Nutrients per Serving:

- Calories 134
- Fat 1 g
- Saturated fat 0 g
- Carbohydrates 27 g
- Fiber 5 g
- Protein 4 g
- Cholesterol 0 mg
- Sugars 16 g
- Sodium 657 mg
- Potassium 404 mg

Garlic Mashed Potatoes with Herbs

Here's something better than your favorite mashed potatoes—mashed potatoes flavored with garlic and herbs. You'll never want to prepare the side dish differently ever again!

Serving Size: 10

Preparation & Cooking Time: 2 hours and 40 minutes

Ingredients:

- 4 lb. potatoes, sliced into cubes
- ½ cup butter, sliced into cubes
- 8 oz. cream cheese, sliced into cubes
- 1 cup sour cream
- ¼ cup heavy whipping cream
- 3 tablespoons fresh chives, minced
- 1 tablespoon fresh parsley, minced
- 3 cloves garlic, minced
- 1 teaspoon fresh thyme, minced
- Salt and pepper to taste

Instructions:

Add the potatoes to a pot.

Pour in the water.

Bring to a boil.

Reduce heat.

Simmer for 15 minutes.

Drain and transfer to a plate.

Mash the potatoes.

Stir in the butter and cream cheese.

Add the remaining ingredients.

Mix well.

Transfer the mixture to your slow cooker.

Cook on low for 3 hours.

Nutrients per Serving:

- Calories 341
- Fat 24 g
- Saturated fat 15 g
- Carbohydrates 26 g
- Fiber 2 g
- Protein 5 g
- Cholesterol 76 mg
- Sugars 3 g
- Sodium 267 mg
- Potassium 813 mg

Lemon Spring Veggies

This dish gives you fresh and colorful vegetables flavored with herbs and lemon zest!

Serving Size: 8

Preparation & Cooking Time: 4 hours and 30 minutes

Ingredients:

- 1 sweet onion, chopped
- 4 carrots, sliced
- 1 ½ lb. baby potatoes, sliced
- 3 tablespoons butter, melted
- Salt and pepper to taste
- 1 cup peas
- 1 teaspoon lemon zest
- ¼ cup chives, minced

Instructions:

Add the onion and carrots to your slow cooker.

Spread the potatoes on top.

Drizzle with the butter.

Season with the salt and pepper.

Cover the pot.

Cook on low for 4 hours.

Stir in the peas.

Cook for 15 more minutes.

Sprinkle with the chives and lemon zest before serving.

Nutrients per Serving:

- Calories 141
- Fat 5 g
- Saturated fat 3 g
- Carbohydrates 23 g
- Fiber 3 g
- Protein 3 g
- Cholesterol 11 mg
- Sugars 5 g
- Sodium 298 mg
- Potassium 520 mg

White Bean & Spinach Soup

Here's a good idea for busy nights. Just prepare the dish early and let your slow cooker do the rest of the work. You can also make a big batch of the soup and freeze each serving in a separate container. Thaw at least the night before, so it's ready to be reheated the next day.

Serving Size: 8

Preparation & Cooking Time: 6 hours and 30 minutes

Ingredients:

- 6 cups vegetable broth
- ½ cup onion, chopped
- 2 cloves garlic, minced
- 15 ½ oz. great northern beans, rinsed and drained
- ½ cup rice
- 15 oz. canned tomato puree
- 1 teaspoon dried basil
- Salt and pepper to taste
- 7 cups spinach, chopped
- ¼ cup Parmesan cheese, shredded

Instructions:

Pour in the vegetable broth.

Add the onion, garlic, great northern beans, rice and tomato puree.

Stir well.

Season with the dried basil, salt and pepper.

Cover the pot.

Cook on low for 6 hours.

Add the spinach.

Cover and cook for 10 minutes.

Sprinkle with the Parmesan cheese before serving.

Nutrients per Serving:

- Calories 151
- Fat 1 g
- Saturated fat 0 g
- Carbohydrates 26 g
- Fiber 5 g
- Protein 7 g
- Cholesterol 2 mg
- Sugars 3 g
- Sodium 291 mg
- Potassium 662 mg

Pumpkin Soup with Lentils

Spices and garlic make this soup extra flavorful. You'll love the creamy and silky texture of both the lentils and soup. The soup pairs well with French bread or cornbread.

Serving Size: 6

Preparation & Cooking Time: 8 hours and 20 minutes

Ingredients:

- 28 oz. vegetable broth
- 1 ½ cups water
- 1 onion, chopped
- 3 cloves garlic, minced
- 1 lb. red potatoes, sliced into cubes
- 1 cup dried lentils, rinsed and drained
- 15 oz. canned pumpkin puree
- ½ teaspoon ground ginger
- Salt and pepper to taste

Instructions:

Pour the vegetable broth and water into your slow cooker.

Stir in the onion and garlic.

Add the red potatoes, dried lentils and pumpkin puree.

Season with the ground ginger, salt and pepper.

Cover the pot.

Cook on low for 8 hours.

Nutrients per Serving:

- Calories 210
- Fat 1 g
- Saturated fat 0 g
- Carbohydrates 42 g
- Fiber 7 g
- Protein 11 g
- Cholesterol 0 mg
- Sugars 5 g
- Sodium 463 mg
- Potassium 221 mg

Slow Cooked Green Beans & Carrots

The combination of butter, tapioca, and sugar adds a unique flavor to fresh vegetables in this quick and simple slow cooker dish.

Serving Size: 8

Preparation & Cooking Time: 7 hours and 20 minutes

Ingredients:

- 2 onions, sliced thinly
- 1 green bell pepper, sliced
- 4 ribs celery, sliced
- 2 tomatoes, sliced
- 4 carrots, sliced
- 2 cups green beans, sliced
- 3 tablespoons tapioca (quick-cooking)
- 1 tablespoon sugar
- ¼ cup butter, melted
- Salt and pepper to taste

Instructions:

Toss the onions, bell pepper, celery, tomatoes, carrots and green beans in your slow cooker.

In a bowl, mix the tapioca, sugar, butter, salt and pepper.

Pour the mixture over the vegetables.

Mix well.

Cover the pot.

Cook on low for 7 hours.

Nutrients per Serving:

- Calories 113
- Fat 6 g
- Saturated fat 4 g
- Carbohydrates 15 g
- Fiber 3 g
- Protein 2 g
- Cholesterol 15 mg
- Sugars 6 g
- Sodium 379 mg
- Potassium 298 mg

Praline Sweet Potatoes

For a change from usual snacks or dinner meals, try topping your sweet potatoes with a mix of butter, flour, sugar and pecans. The result is the melding of delicious flavors and textures.

Serving Size: 6

Preparation & Cooking Time: 4 hours and 30 minutes

Ingredients:

- Cooking spray
- ¼ cup butter, melted
- 3 cups sweet potatoes, cooked and mashed
- 3 eggs, beaten
- 1 cup sugar
- ½ cup milk
- 1 teaspoon vanilla extract
- Salt to taste

Topping

- ¼ cup all-purpose flour
- ½ cup pecans
- ½ cup brown sugar
- 2 tablespoons cold butter, sliced into cubes

Instructions:

Spray your slow cooker with oil.

Add the butter, sweet potatoes, eggs, sugar, milk, vanilla extract and salt to the pot.

Mix well.

Cook on low for 3 hours.

Combine the flour, pecans and sugar.

Fold in the butter.

Stir until crumbly.

Sprinkle the topping over the sweet potatoes.

Cover the pot.

Cook on low for 1 hour.

Nutrients per Serving:

- Calories 556
- Fat 21 g
- Saturated fat 9 g
- Carbohydrates 87 g
- Fiber 5 g
- Protein 8 g
- Cholesterol 125 mg
- Sugars 62 g
- Sodium 580 mg
- Potassium 656 mg

Artichoke Cream Dip

Yes, you can incredibly make a delicious dip for your tortilla chips or crackers using artichokes. Here's the simple recipe to follow.

Serving Size: 10

Preparation & Cooking Time: 1 hour and 20 minutes

Ingredients:

- 28 oz. canned artichoke hearts, chopped
- ½ cup Swiss cheese, shredded
- 8 oz. cream cheese, sliced into cubes
- 2 cups mozzarella cheese, shredded
- ½ cup mayonnaise
- 1 cup Parmesan cheese, shredded
- 2 tablespoons lemon juice
- 2 tablespoons yogurt
- 1 tablespoon jalapeno pepper, chopped
- 1 teaspoon garlic powder
- Salt to taste
- Tortilla chips

Instructions:

Add all of the ingredients except the tortilla chips to your slow cooker.

Cover the pot.

Cook on low for 1 hour.

Serve with the tortilla chips.

Nutrients per Serving:

- Calories 152
- Fat 12 g
- Saturated fat 5 g
- Carbohydrates 4 g
- Fiber 0 g
- Protein 7 g
- Cholesterol 27 mg
- Sugars 1 g
- Sodium 519 mg
- Potassium 341 mg

Split Pea Soup

This easy and simple pea soup recipe will be a go-to dish for your busy days. It's delicious. It fills you up. But it doesn't take too much effort to prepare.

Serving Size: 8

Preparation & Cooking Time: 7 hours and 10 minutes

Ingredients:

- 6 cups water
- 1 onion, chopped
- 1 rib celery, chopped
- 1 carrot, chopped
- 16 oz. dried green split peas, rinsed and drained
- 1 bay leaf
- ½ teaspoon dried thyme
- Salt and pepper to taste

Instructions:

Mix all of the ingredients in your slow cooker.

Cover the pot.

Cook on low for 7 hours.

Discard the bay leaf before serving.

Nutrients per Serving:

- Calories 202
- Fat 1 g
- Saturated fat 9 g
- Carbohydrates 36 g
- Fiber 15 g
- Protein 14 g
- Cholesterol 0 mg
- Sugars 5 g
- Sodium 462 mg
- Potassium 603 mg

Bulgur & Beans

Combine bulgur and beans in your slow cooker and add some spices, sugar and tomatoes. You get a meal that's not only filling but also wows you with its great flavors.

Serving Size: 10

Preparation & Cooking Time: 3 hours and 40 minutes

Ingredients:

- 3 tablespoons vegetable oil, divided
- 2 onions, chopped
- 1 sweet red pepper, chopped
- 5 cloves garlic, minced
- 2 teaspoons ground ginger
- 1 tablespoon paprika
- ½ teaspoon cayenne pepper
- 1 tablespoon ground cumin
- ½ teaspoon ground cinnamon
- Pepper to taste
- 1 ½ cups bulgur
- 28 oz. canned crushed tomatoes
- 14 oz. canned diced tomatoes
- 32 oz. vegetable broth
- 2 tablespoons brown sugar
- 2 tablespoons soy sauce
- 15 oz. chickpeas, rinsed and drained
- ½ cup golden raisins
- Chopped fresh cilantro

Instructions:

Add 2 tablespoons of the vegetable oil to a pan over medium heat.

Cook the onions and sweet red pepper for 3 minutes, stirring often.

Stir in the garlic, ground ginger, paprika, cayenne pepper, ground cumin, ground cinnamon and pepper.

Cook for 1 minute.

Transfer the mixture to your slow cooker.

Add the remaining oil to your pan.

Cook the bulgur for 3 minutes.

Transfer to the pot.

Stir in the rest of the ingredients.

Cover the pot.

Cook on low for 3 hours.

Stir in the raisins and chickpeas.

Cook for 30 minutes.

Sprinkle with the cilantro.

Nutrients per Serving:

- Calories 245
- Fat 6 g
- Saturated fat 0 g
- Carbohydrates 45 g
- Fiber 8 g
- Protein 8 g
- Cholesterol 0 mg
- Sugars 15 g
- Sodium 752 mg
- Potassium 881 mg

Mexican Fondue

This is the Mexican version of the popular Swiss cheese dish. For sure, you're going to enjoy preparing and serving it to your family and friends.

Serving Size: 8

Preparation & Cooking Time: 1 hour and 45 minutes

Ingredients:

- 14 ½ oz. canned diced tomatoes
- 3 tablespoons green chili, chopped
- 14 ¾ oz. cream style corn
- 1 teaspoon chili powder
- 16 oz. process cheese, sliced into cubes
- French bread, sliced into cubes

Instructions:

In a bowl, mix the tomatoes, green chili, cream style corn and chili powder.

Pour the mixture into your slow cooker.

Stir in the cheese.

Cover the pot.

Cook on high for 1 hour and 30 minutes, stirring every 20 to 30 minutes.

Serve with the bread slices.

Nutrients per Serving:

- Calories 105
- Fat 6 g
- Saturated fat 4 g
- Carbohydrates 7 g
- Fiber 1 g
- Protein 5 g
- Cholesterol 20 mg
- Sugars 3 g
- Sodium 421 mg
- Potassium 516 mg

Cauliflower Korma

Korma is an Indian dish that's made by braising meats or vegetables in a sauce with cream or yogurt. In this recipe, we make cauliflower korma that's simply irresistible.

Serving Size: 4

Preparation & Cooking Time: 5 hours and 20 minutes

Ingredients:

- ½ cup tomato puree
- ¼ cup korma curry paste
- 2 cups vegetable broth
- 1 cauliflower, trimmed
- ¼ cup Greek style plain yogurt
- ¼ cup cream
- 2 teaspoons corn flour
- Almonds, slivered
- 1 tomato, chopped
- Green chili, sliced

Instructions:

Combine the tomato puree, korma curry paste and vegetable broth in your slow cooker.

Add the cauliflower and turn to coat evenly with the sauce.

Cook on low for 5 hours.

Mix the yogurt, cream and flour in another bowl.

Add the mixture to the pot.

Cook for 10 more minutes.

Serve with the almonds, tomato and green chili.

Nutrients per Serving:

- Calories 145
- Fat 4 g
- Saturated Fat 1.7 g
- Carbohydrate 21.3 g
- Fiber 6.3 g
- Protein 9.4 g
- Cholesterol 7 mg
- Sugars 8.4 g
- Sodium 546 mg
- Potassium 925 mg

Conclusion

No matter what variations of a plant-based diet have been shown to have many health benefits such as strengthening our body's immunity from various diseases and lowering the risk of developing serious illnesses.

One great example of the ideal plant-based diet is the Mediterranean diet that has been around for decades and still remains as one of the healthiest diets in existence.

Get to try all of the amazing plant-based recipes in this cookbook and be inspired to come up with your very own recipes in the future.

Author's Afterthoughts

I want to convey my big thanks to all of my readers who have taken the time to read my book. Readers like you make my work so rewarding and I cherish each and every one of you.

Grateful cannot describe how I feel when I know that someone has chosen my work over all of the choices available online. I hope you enjoyed the book as much as I enjoyed writing it.

Feedback from my readers is how I grow and learn as a chef and an author. Please take the time to let me know your thoughts by leaving a review on Amazon so I and your fellow readers can learn from your experience.

My deepest thanks,

Sophia Freeman

https://sophia.subscribemenow.com/

* * * * * ★ ★ ★ ★ ★ * * * *

Printed in Great Britain
by Amazon